Essays on Dual

Minou Bahram

The cover image depicts a woman with tattoos of Iranian symbols and words signifying the indelible marks of her origin.

The paisleys and the cursive, Eslimi design on the woman's back are decorative elements of Iranian art as is the Shah Abbas flower on her leg.

The words on her upper arm are 'Woman, Life, Freedom' in Persian.

The flower on her shoulder is a lotus flower which appears as it is on the stone carvings of Persepolis.

The woman is sitting amongst the British countryside surrounded with green rolling hills.

Cover Illustration by the author

Essays

Āberū   p.5

Maman   p.21

Affinity   p.45

Photographs

Maman in 1956 – aged 19   p.22

'The Elephant' on the record cover

for Shahr-e Qesseh.   p.46

Āberū

با من ای هموطن

سخن مرا بگوی

در دل هرسخن

هدف مرا بجوی

حرف ما را ببر به سراسر جهان

ما که جان می دهیم به بهای آبرو

Oh, people of my homeland

Speak with me, tell my story

In the essence of all that you say

Seek my aspiration

Spread our message all over the world

We are the ones who give our lives in return for āberū

By Fereydoun Farrokhzad (1938 – 1992)

My Very Personal Debt to the Brave People of Iran

There is a concept called āberū in Persian culture. The word is often translated as 'reputation' in English. If you have no āberū, you have lost face. You are a disgrace to your family and the people you represent. Iranians are raised to preserve the āberū of their family and those connected to them.

I am sure all nations with a history of many thousands of years carry this kind of pride. At any rate, when I arrived in Britain in 1985 - at the age of seventeen, I was proud of my heritage, and I cared about how other people perceived me. At the same time, my parents who sent me here to study, had told me not to tell anyone that I was Iranian. They were afraid that I would be judged a terrorist.

Sadly, their fears were well-founded. I cannot count the number of times that I have had to explain myself to people once they found out that I came from Iran. It has been a fact of life for Iranians abroad that they have often had to clarify their allegiances before people of their adopted country can trust them.

The absurdity of this situation is that of course the great majority of Iranians who have left Iran have been fleeing the regime. An Iranian woman without hijab abroad, clearly has no connections with the regime. And yet, we have constantly had to explain to people that we are not what they thought we were – our own nemesis. All this explaining does take a toll on the psyche. You end up feeling unwanted in the country where you have taken refuge. It is like a Jewish German person during WWII having to explain constantly that they are not a Nazi just because they were born in Germany.

Edinburgh was the first British city that I lived in. I did my A-levels there, then I got into Cambridge University after two years of living in a foreign culture, a cold climate and washing, cleaning and cooking for myself. That is some achievement. But at the time, I didn't think about patting myself on the back. My mother and my sister were still in Iran, being bombed by Iraqi planes. Telephone connections were erratic at best. I worried a lot about their safety.

Both my parents lost their jobs in the aftermath of the 1979 revolution. They had supported the overthrow of the Shah but in the process had become known as active members of the secular opposition who wanted democracy and not Islamist rule for Iran. We had also been war refugees and had ended up in Tehran until finally my father was able to find a job abroad. My mother and my sister remained in Iran, and I was sent to Britain.

My mother had never worn the hijab until it was made compulsory a few years after the revolution. Her father was also a secular man whose only religion was a belief in a loving God. He had sent all three of his daughters to university and was proud that they were not veiled. No one had any problem with eating pork or drinking wine in my family.

One day, when I was twelve years old, I went out with my dad wearing denim dungarees and a T-shirt. This was shortly after we arrived in Tehran during the Iran-Iraq war. When we came back, someone had sprayed 'death to the unveiled' – in red, all over our wall. That was the day my dad said that I had no choice. Our neighbours opposite were Revolutionary Guards – Guardians of the Islamic Republic. Dad said to wear a scarf. Then we heard of acid attacks on women without a hijab.

We moved house later and lived in a tall apartment block. One day we could see hundreds of men on motor bikes in the street below. They were attacking women. A friend we were expecting arrived. He was a young man. He was covered in cuts and his clothes were torn. He said he had been trying to save the women and fending off the attackers on motorbikes. They had acid and they had knives. He said that taxi drivers were helping by stopping for the women.

At school, we were searched every day for 'items of make-up etc.' We were constantly watched. If our behaviour was not 'Islamic' enough, we would receive low marks on our report card for 'Discipline.' This meant that our chances of entering university were jeopardised. We were put in a bus every year on the anniversary of the attack on the American Embassy. Then we had to stand outside the embassy building and shout 'death to' just about everything and everybody. We were being watched while this went on as well. We feared what could happen to our families if we did not comply.

This was while we all remembered when the US embassy was stormed on 4 November 1979 and its staff were taken hostage by Islamist students, and how upset we were at school. My classmates were all saying how embarrassed and ashamed their parents were. How this act had not left us any āberū in the world.

You may not know that while the US hostages appeared on world media every day for the next four-hundred-and-forty-four days, the regime had set about executing all secular and left-wing opposition and even other Islamists who were not part of their gang. Kurdistan was particularly hard hit as the province rejected the rule of the Islamic Republic. It is estimated that at least ten thousand Iranian Kurds were massacred during the early years of the 1979 revolution and an estimated twelve thousand Iranians were executed elsewhere. We had no āberū in the world. We were being massacred inside the country while the rest of the world chose to perceive us as crazy flag burners, hostage takers and terrorists. There was little effort by western media or western governments to separate the people of Iran from the regime, its cronies, and its aggressive foreign policies.

*****

The people who supported the 1979 revolution did not see the Islamic Republic coming. It is commonly said that the revolution was hijacked. The mass killings in the early 1980s by the regime were against people who had supported that revolution but were not loyal to the Islamic Republic. Thousands more were executed in 1988 by the order of Ayatollah Khomeini. These killings, together with the mayhem and horror of the Iran-Iraq war where hundreds of thousands died, put an indescribable fear into the heart of every Iranian. Traumatised by the death of their loved ones, the generations who remembered the 1979 revolution, focused on bringing up their children to know that it was not right to live with gender apartheid, it was not right to constantly fear for your safety, and it was not right to live with poverty or the corruption of the regime and its hostile foreign policy.

These children rose up against the regime in their own way. There were uprisings in 1999, 2009, and every year from 2016 to 2021. Each time, people were arrested, tortured, killed on the streets, or executed. In November 2019 alone, fifteen hundred were killed over three days. Then, of course, there was the downing of the Ukraine Air passenger plane PS752 by the IRGC resulting in the death of all one-hundred-and-seventy-six people on board.

*****

My personal story is that of a family of my father's cousins in the early 1980s. Two girls in their twenties were executed. Their crime was that they were members of a communist party. Their mother died of a heart attack on the day they were arrested. One of them was married and her husband was also executed. The family was asked to pay for the bullets that had killed the girls or else they would not be given the bodies. Of the girls' brothers, one fled Iran but died as a result of a chemical gas attack by Saddam Hussein's regime. Another brother had the task of burying his sisters with his own hands. He was never the same after that. He died in his early sixties.

*****

One memory that I revisit, is the day I arrived at my college in Cambridge, having had to physically get there on my own. I had five boxes, a guitar and a suitcase and I had to negotiate my way from Edinburgh to Cambridge on the train.

The train journey involves changing trains once, so I had these scary few moments where I had to rapidly get all the boxes onto the platform in Peterborough and then find a trolley to put them on, then run to the next train, load the boxes on and again in Cambridge, take the boxes off before the train moved off. Then catch a minibus to my college.

I was looking haggard. I weighed only forty-eight kilogrammes. I was a tiny kid, a 19-year-old carrying all these boxes, they were heavy because they mostly contained books. Anyway, I got these to the college in the minibus. I took them off the minibus then took them to the Porters' Lodge and explained who I was. They told me where I had to go. This was about a ten-minute walk - a long way with all those boxes. I got to the bottom of the staircase and realised my room was on the third floor. I carried everything upstairs until I had only two boxes left.

Other people were arriving completely relaxed with their parents. Both parents were helping them settle and were carrying their stuff up for them. That is what normal people do after all. Then somebody's dad offered to take one of my boxes for me. I was grateful. When he got to the top landing, he said, 'Where are you from?' I said, 'Oh, I'm from Iran'. And he said, 'What have you got in there? bombs? Ha ha ha ha'.

I just felt so sad. I was so tired. I was so hungry. So hassled out of my brain. My sister and my mother were being bombed. I had lived under bombs myself. And I was being asked if I carried bombs.

*****

There are many similar stories to tell. There was that time when an American guy said to me at a Christmas dinner, 'So, you're from Iran. No offence, but I hate terrorism'. Or when I was plunged into a deep depression because of racist behaviour at my place of work. The number of times I had to explain to the same person that I was not an Arab. The number of times I have had to tell people that the world's first written declaration of human rights was issued by an Iranian king close to three thousand years ago just so they know I care about human rights.

This article is not the place for detailed descriptions of every single incident of discrimination I have come across because its main aim is to thank the brave people of Iran for 'buying my āberū'. It is bad enough to be misunderstood in this extreme way but when you have the added pressure of protecting your āberū', that is another whole layer of mental anguish.

This is why the Woman-Life-Freedom movement in Iran has been momentous for me personally and for all dual national Iranians abroad in more ways than one. The young women and men, teenagers and all those on the streets in Iran have done things that had been far beyond the reach of any imagination for over forty-three years. I never thought that this would happen; that one day I would not have to explain to British people that I am not a terrorist; that they will just see with their own eyes; that there will be evidence in world media everywhere. That they will see the real Iran. This is what Iranians are really like, and that we have been victims of this regime many thousands of times more than anyone in the West.

After living in Britain for close to forty years, I finally feel like a weight has lifted from my shoulders. I feel I can hold my head up high and be proud of who I am. My other dual national Iranian-British friends feel the same. This feeling of pride, the feeling of being understood is a huge gift from the amazing people in Iran who are putting their lives on the line. They are healing the wounds of their entire nation, inside and outside of the country.

The world should take heed that the people of Iran want a regime change and a revolution is in the making. This, history's first women's revolution, will change the face of the world for the better in many, many ways. In this day and age of countless doomsday scenarios, the news from Iran is a ray of light and a beacon of hope to behold. Support the people of Iran so that you are a part of history, so that you can be proud of your stance against oppression for years to come.

Epilogue – July 2023

The last few pages were written during 2022, when the Woman-Life-Freedom movement was in full swing.

At the time of writing, the Iranian people continue their struggle against injustice, but this is no longer newsworthy in the West. Constant internet outages in Iran and the lack of access by Western media to the country have not helped matters.

Many thousands are imprisoned or have been killed. Understandably, there is a temporary halt in mass uprisings.

Meanwhile, the eight million dual Iranian nationals all over the world continue to follow the news from Iran on a daily basis. All Iranians continue to hope and dream of freedom. The people's resolve has not died.

The events of late 2022 and early 2023, constituted the most prolonged period of unrest in Iran since the 1979 revolution. I do hope that the general public in western countries continue to remember the beautiful young people who gave their lives on the streets in the months following the death of Mahsa Amini. These brave people showed the true face of Iran to the rest of the world in an unprecedented way.

The feelings of elation and the vindication Iranians felt during those heady months of protest, and their powerful hope for a bright future were shared with many in the West.

But how constant is the memory of Western society? More importantly, does it matter if people outside Iran revert to their old ways having forgotten the events of 2022 and early 2023?

This is the dichotomy that āberū creates within Iranians.

On the one hand, when the word āberū is associated with dignity and personal pride, its existence as a concept, multiplies the empowering feeling that a person experiences when they know that others respect and understand them correctly.

Of course, this also means that being misjudged as inferior or defective can become more challenging to accept for Iranians. This reaction in itself is not a bad thing. It is perhaps one reason for Iranians being vocal about injustice throughout their history.

On the other hand, in its totally negative form, the notion of āberū affords an unnatural weight to opinions of others about a person.

Like all Iranians, I have experienced or observed these negative effects too often and they can be corrosive.

Examples that come to mind are families enforcing rigid controls over their children's choice of career or spouse, people not speaking up against domestic violence and people keeping up appearances when they cannot afford to do so – all to project an 'acceptable' image of the family.

During the protests of last year and early this year, many Iranian friends expressed the same sentiments that I described earlier in this essay. We were able to feel understood for a few months at least. We were able to be proud to identify as Iranian rather than feel anxious or ashamed about the way our country of birth was perceived.

The positive effects of those few months continue to influence the way I react to my surroundings. I do wonder whether having lived outside Iran for so long had made me doubt my own convictions about the people of Iran.

There was a sense of hopelessness that used to fly past like a dark shadow as I sometimes wondered whether Iranians living in Iran saw immigration as the only way out of oppression. That dark shadow is now gone.

I know now that the love for Iran that I have felt all my life is etched in the hearts of the great majority of Iranian people. This love has not been undermined by ideology or oppression as I had feared.

This love now sustains the Woman-Life-Freedom movement. The events of last year have not only given Iranians hope, but they have also revived a sense of belonging and unity that overcomes the need to care about how we are perceived by others.

Maman

My grandfather - my mother's father - the son of Iranian nomads, had lost both his parents by the age of seven. But he managed to teach himself to read and write and later made sure that all five of his children, including his three daughters, went to university.

My mother was his eldest child. She studied biology at Tehran University then became a high-school teacher and later head teacher and school inspector. Maman was born in 1937 in Iran. It is a source of pride for me that she was an accomplished woman for her generation and her father was a progressive man for his time.

From what I have heard and the photographs I have seen, Maman was beautiful, funny, and clever as a young single woman. She used to make her own clothes. She was a size eight and one-hundred-and-sixty cm tall. Her sisters say that she had a lot of suitors, but she turned them all down until father came along. My parents were colleagues at the same school and only six months apart in age - father being older.

I remember my mother when she had just turned forty. It was two years before the 1979 revolution, and I was nine years old. She was then a confident career woman. She was a size fourteen by then, and she still dressed well. Lots of other adults looked up to her. She was well known and respected in our town. Outside our home, she knew how to handle people and situations. I felt safe when she was around.

As with all people, certain endearing memories of Maman have stayed with me.

Once when I was ten years old, I told my teacher that my grandfather had died. This was just because I hadn't done my homework. The teacher saw Maman afterwards and gave his condolences. My mother just said thank you quietly and then, told me off about lying, in the car on the way home. I have always remembered this and been grateful to her.

Our father was not around much when we were small. He was always studying either abroad or in other cities in Iran. Maman brought us up as a single working parent for most of my childhood. When we were young, she was just about able to cope. All the years that father was away, she handled everything. I don't remember missing my father at all.

We rarely went on holiday as a family with father. The usual summer holiday consisted of Maman piling the three of us in the car at 4:00 a.m. and driving one thousand km to Tehran in one day. We lived in the South of Iran then and my mother's parents and siblings all lived in Tehran.

Maman would rest her left elbow in the open car window and drive one-handed. By the time we got to Tehran she would always have a sun-burnt left arm. Those holidays were the happiest time of the year for the four of us. I felt loved by my mother and her family, and I remember the love I had for her as well.

Then the 1979 revolution happened.

Maman lost her job after the revolution because she 'had disrespected Mohammad the prophet.' Father also lost his job because he had been pro-revolution but anti-religion. He had given one too many public speeches in support of his secular social-democratic ideals.

When the war with Iraq broke out in 1980, we also became war refugees as our town was too near to the Iraqi border. Father became more violent and unpleasant than before as he tried to cope with the pressures of supporting a family with no prospect of a job in a country where there was no social security and where the government had closed the borders. He was like a caged animal in those days.

Maman was not able to work anymore as a schoolteacher either. She had been forced to retire because the religious studies teacher at her school had reported her to the authorities. She never worked again after that.

The vibrant, funny woman faded away over the years. She tried to cope with father's temper tantrums and verbal humiliation and keep the family going. She didn't particularly like father, or she said that she didn't. But we always knew that she loved him. She had chosen him over all those other suitors after all. I have to say that this love faded over the years. That is what happens to love when it is not nurtured. There was just some of it left by the time Maman died. Maybe some of her love for her children also died with the passing of time. Depression was beginning to take hold.

She was at her happiest and most natural when father wasn't around. He eventually managed to leave Iran and work with his brother as an accountant for the family business. He used to send money home to us. We would see him a couple of times a year when we went abroad and that was OK but when he occasionally came to Iran, I found his presence hard to bear.

In contrast, Maman was so different in that it was easy to relax with her when father was not around. Even at the worst of times her sense of humour often found a way to shine through. I remember her moments of happiness with great affection. She used to have sayings and proverbs for all sorts of occasions. She had a great memory for jokes and could accurately mimic every regional accent in Iran. She could also whistle loudly with two fingers in her mouth. She used this whistle to hail taxis sometimes.

My parents' relationship was not equal. Maman would let father get away with too much. Her attitude with father was 'Let's not rock the boat' at any cost. So, if he mistreated us, we sometimes got 'why did you have to go and upset your father again?' or if the abuse got really bad, she would swear she would leave him but never did. As far as I know, she never even mentioned leaving him to his face.

I was not allowed to object when father decided that I had to go to Britain to study, I told my mother that I didn't want to go but she said I would be throwing my life away if I stayed. She said that I would be condemning myself to a university education full of religious nonsense.

She also quoted her own mother – a woman who also had a saying for every occasion, 'Don't be like that boy who was clicking his fingers and dancing in the street and when people asked him why he was so happy, he said that he had got himself buggered to spite his father.' There was some logic in this as one of my reasons for not wanting to go was that I knew my father would be forever reminding me that I owed him because of the money he had spent on sending me away.

In the end I did go. I also did get constant reminders of how much I was costing my father. Although he has now stopped talking about that.

My older sister had already been there for a year. We were both seventeen when we were sent out. We had no family nearby but knew English well. We went from an existence of being looked after by our mother at home to having to do everything for ourselves. Back in Iran, my mother lived with our younger sister. I am sure she missed us terribly. But she never told us that she did. In fact, we hardly had much contact with her after we left. This was partly because of bad telephone lines but also because father had decided that telephone calls were too expensive and Maman as always, didn't argue. She didn't write to us either.

*****

After she died, while I was clearing up her room, I found a poem that she had scribbled on a piece of paper.

'You are so good and so dear that I do not dare entrust you to God when we part'.

آنقدر خوب و عزیزی که به هنگام وداع،
حیفم آید که تو را دست خدا بسپارم

I cried because I felt she had written this for her children.

In our absence, Maman had tried to fill the gap by mothering other people, sometimes strangers, sometimes cousins, sometimes children of cousins.
At her funeral, so many people came up to me and said that she was a mother to them. Apparently, she had called everyone 'my child.' She had nursed people through depression, flu, shingles, etc. A voice inside me screamed 'she never did any of that for ME and she was supposed to be MY mother.'

Of course, I remember times when she was loving. As a child, I knew that she loved me. But once I left Iran, it was as if I ceased to exist for her. She would come to visit with or without father once every two or three years, but it was never like the old times.

Over the years I have concluded that she chose what she thought was the easiest way for herself to cope with our absence. She chose not to think of us, and any contact would have been a reminder, so she created a life without us for herself to keep her pain away. But then, what were we supposed to do with our pain?

There was not much contact in between visits. Sometimes there would be a birthday phone call but even that was not guaranteed. When we did meet, a lot of our conversations centred around how awful father was. I felt frustrated because ultimately, when it came to father, I couldn't do much for her. The few times I had tried to stand up to my father had gone badly.

She would not leave him or argue with him. She used to say that silent treatment is the best way. But it wasn't really, and she knew it. She just didn't stand up for herself or her children and caused herself – and us - a lot of harm in the process. My lesson from this has been to be different with my kids. That's a good thing.

When I feel sad about how she could have had a happier life, I remind myself of her sound, unpretentious moral values, and good qualities. She was funny, quite the feminist and loved small, delicate things. She loved reading and then teaching you the stuff that she had read about. I've got all of that from her, plus a large bank of jokes and anecdotes.

She used to make wine in her cellar in Tehran. This was of course illegal activity but not an uncommon hobby in Iran given the lack of availability of wine. The grape seller in the bazaar would keep crates of grapes for her and always say with a big wink 'These are really good for VINEGAR you know'.

Another time we laughed a lot when she had gone to the other side of Tehran on the bus to cash in all her seafood war rations during the Iran-Iraq war. She was given a huge frozen fish as tall as herself because she hadn't been in to claim seafood rations for some months. On the way back, she said she had sat the fish next to her on the bus and was asked by a man in shabby clothes whether she'd been on a whale hunt. 'Hey lady, have you been hunting whales today?'

She had a lovely spirit, just quite a timid one. Then she married a man who was just so wrong for her, and she didn't have the strength or circumstances to walk away. She cared too much about what other people thought. That's another thing that I have learnt not to do in life.

Loqman was asked: How did you learn your manners? He said: I learnt my manners from those who were without any. Whatever they did, I did not do.

لقمان را گفتند ادب از که آموختی؟
گفت از بی ادبان.
هر چه از ایشان در نظر ناپسند آمد، از فعل آن پرهیز کردم.

My mother lived the way she did because she was unable to live any other way. That doesn't make her a bad person, just not a very 'flexible' one. Her only mode of operation seems to have been to just stay true to her upbringing.

It was a mixture of fear and pride that guided her through life. She was so fearful of change – maybe because of all the change that had foisted itself upon her - that she didn't want to take any risks. Leaving father would have been a huge risk in her eyes both financially and in terms of her standing in society. I must avoid fear of the unknown. It's debilitating.

Pride is a common feature amongst nations with an ancient past. Persian pride can be - to my mind, quite unreasonably oversized. My mother, unlike many of her peers, had chosen father herself. There was no arranged marriage or family pressure. I do feel that she thought that if she left father, she would be admitting to having made a mistake and she didn't want to do that. My mother's pride also kept her from considering any other work than teaching in a formal government setting after she was forced to retire.

I once heard a woman on TV say that 'When you suffer in life, it's because you are not following your destiny.' Maybe my mother was going against her destiny?

The Death of My Mother

It's such a bloody hard thing to come to terms with. She was my anchor until I left Iran in 1985. Then, she suddenly disappeared from my life. In a way, that was when I really lost her. Especially now that I am a mother myself, I cannot understand why she didn't insist on coming to Britain with us.

Perhaps she was too afraid of father; far too afraid. After she lost her job, she would not disobey him at any cost. And he was oh so bad at making decisions. He said once that she shouldn't go because she would just be spending his money having the time of her life in Britain and that was enough to put her off. She didn't fight or even argue for her right to be with her children. She was so proud that she didn't want to ask him for anything that he didn't want to give and particularly not money.

She used to often say out loud that she wished she would die and be rid of father. One time I got so angry with her that I said 'Why don't you wish for him to die? Why do you keep wishing yourself dead?' She had no answer.

We told her it was depression, but she wouldn't go to therapy or take any medication. She said she didn't want people to think that she was crazy...But most of all I think she didn't want to think she was crazy herself.

She wouldn't go to any doctors in fact. She didn't know that her cholesterol and her blood sugar were both dangerously high. We found that out when she was dying. She also didn't know that she had advanced lung cancer. She knew about an aneurism that she had but had refused an operation. Her sister said - and I agree – that she wanted to die. She just slowly killed herself. This thought has made me terribly sad.

She died in the intensive care ward of one of the best hospitals in Tehran. I arrived in Tehran at 2:00 a.m. with eight hours' notice and was by her bedside by 3:30a.m. My older sister couldn't come. She was all wired up and did not move when I talked to her. She was in a coma.

We received a phone call three days later when we had just rushed home to change clothes and eat something. The nurse said: "You'd better come over quickly. Your mother only has minutes to live." But we were at least forty-five minutes away by car. She died on her own fifteen minutes before we got there.

Her sister had arrived earlier because she lived closer to the hospital. My aunt said we had to prepare ourselves because they had already wrapped her in a shroud...

I will never forget that awful scene. It was like something out of a horror movie. My mother on her hospital bed, in a shroud with only her face showing... Her body was still warm. Why had they done this?

Maybe this is what happens when people are deprived of the freedom to express healthy emotions because of the pervasive controls of the Islamic Republic. Maybe fear has become the only permitted emotion and so various degrees of it are normalised. These thoughts were with me during my time in Iran while the events of the following few days reduced me to a shaking wreck.

My Mother's Burial

For the entire Muslim population of Tehran - some twelve million people, there is one main cemetery. As you would imagine, this place is a Metropolis in its own right. The main street in Behesht-e Zahra (Zahra's Paradise, Zahra being the eldest daughter of the Prophet Mohammad) is an eight-lane motorway. There is a whole huge area devoted to the dead from the Iran-Iraq war. There is a section with unmarked graves for political prisoners and there are streets upon streets of graves. You need a map and an exact address to be able to find a grave and you must drive to get there. There are even 'posh' streets where richer people have mausoleums for all the dead in their families.

I should say here that I had never been to a burial before in Iran. My mother wouldn't let me go to burials. She used to say they were traumatic. Last time she came to visit me, she said it would be nice to die in England so she could be cremated.

She would have liked to have been buried in her best clothes with her hair looking nice and no hijab in sight. She called her scarf 'My Islam.' My mother had never worn a hijab until it was made compulsory after the 1979 revolution, and she so disliked having to wear it.

This is how it came to be that my mother's burial was the first Shi'a burial I ever saw. And I thought of how hard life in Iran is when people can't even choose how they are buried.

We all arrived at the graveyard in a bus. The place was absolutely crowded with relatives and friends of the dead. There were men going around with placards holding the name of the deceased above their heads, very much like tour guides in Rome or Paris or London advertising their names. Our group gathered around the guy holding Maman's name up and we waited for the body to be brought out of the 'ablution room' – where it had been washed.

Once every five to ten minutes, a body would come out of an opening in the wall which was connected to this ablution room. The name of the deceased would be shouted out and male relatives would gather and take away the body, which was wrapped in a shroud, and placed in a covered, dark green plastic stretcher, while chanting la-ilaha-illa-Allah. There was something very moving about this part of the ceremony. I felt that my mother was supported by the men in her family at last. She would have liked that idea.

Maman's body came out. My cousins, Maman's cousins, uncles, and other men I had not seen for almost thirty years, swept up the stretcher and walked off to another large hall next door. They put the body down and a mulla appeared.

The mulla said that my younger sister and I had to identify the body at this point. He said it was an administrative issue. They had bodies mixed up before and now the procedure was for her children to unwrap the face and make sure it's the correct body. I had been warned about this but was still not prepared for it. Why wouldn't they tag the bodies? Fear is their best friend.

With trembling fingers, my sister and I tried to undo the tough knots that they had tied around the neck and finally got through. My sister was crying quite a lot, but I was just shaking. We took the bandage off the face but there was a layer of cotton wool under that on the eyes.

At that point I thought: What if this isn't my mother? We pried the cotton off carefully and it was Maman. My sister just cried so loud and so hard. She kept saying, 'It's her, It's her, It's her...' Then we covered the face as well as we could and stepped away.

The mulla was getting impatient. He said he had to recite the prayer of the dead. He shouted out that all women had to go and stand behind the men. These were men we had been hugging and kissing only a couple of hours before at home. He kept ordering my sister and I about. I just wanted to tell him to 'piss off.'

He said his prayer and then the body was picked up again and taken to a van waiting outside to be driven to the graveside. Our bus followed. There were about sixty people at the graveside altogether.

My father was not allowed to touch my mother after she died. I learnt that once your spouse dies, you become haram, forbidden, to each-other as if you were total strangers.

The point here was that they required someone strong enough and tall enough to go and stand in the grave and lower the body into the grave. This person had to be mahram meaning she or he had to be allowed to touch my mother.

My sister and I couldn't do it. The grave was six feet deep, and we couldn't physically hold the body and lower it and climb out. So, the only person available was my brother-in-law, my sister's husband.

He was crying his eyes out as he received the body and then the mulla said that he had to stay in the grave, unwrap the face, face the body towards

Mecca, bend over and continue shaking the body until the mulla's prayers were finished. Such unnecessary trauma.

My brother-in-law stayed in the grave but was begging quietly to be allowed to cover the face quickly. I told him to just do it. The mulla was too far to see what he was doing anyway. Then all I remember was my brother-in-law repeating quietly and in English, 'When can I come out?'
It took the mulla a very long ten minutes to finish his prayers, at which point, he said in a loud voice, 'Let us all say praise to the Prophet Mohammad and his descendants.' Usually, the response to this call is a loud chorus of praise but everyone kept quiet. The mulla repeated his request but still not a peep. Finally, he said, 'There must be at least sixty people here and no one is saying praise to the Prophet?' Still not a sound... I thought my mother would have liked that. Although I am sure some people would have said the praise in their hearts, no one said it aloud. It was the only protest we felt we were able to make. The only way we tried to register that we had not wanted a funeral like this for Maman. That she wouldn't have wanted a funeral like this.
My father has of course survived Maman. She got her wish. She died before him.

Despite our differences, I do love my father just as I love my mother still. I like hearing father's voice on the telephone. He calls me his 'wise' daughter when he is in a good mood. Father is old now and has mellowed somewhat but the young angry man bursts out now and then. Now that he is weaker, not being physically afraid of him helps. It also helps to know that my mother does not have to suffer his temper anymore.

As with all Iranians of my generation, I can't help but think how we would have fared if the 1979 revolution had not happened. Whether my parents would have found happiness together or gone their separate ways. Either way, I think it is absolutely true to say that they would both have had happier lives.

Affinity

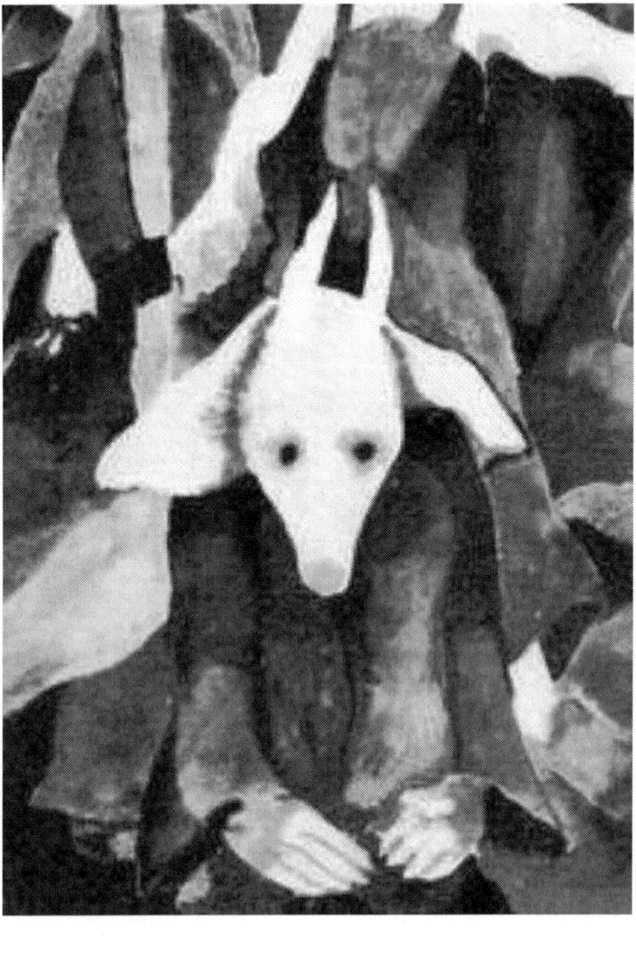

Such great pity for Iran to become a ruin!
And for her to become the den of leopards and lions

Abolqasem Ferdowsi (940 – 1025 CE)

دریغ است ایران که ویران شود
کنام پلنگان و شیران شود

The Motherland

The verses above are known by all Iranians. In fact, I cannot remember when I first learnt them. As a child, I used to deliberately give myself the shivers by imagining wild animals roaming around ruined Iranian cities of old. It was a terrifying thought.

And yet, many such wild beasts have ravaged Iran throughout its three-thousand-year history and the people of Iran have endured while fiercely protecting their Persian identity. Their culture has won the battle in every instance.

The Greeks, under Alexander (356 – 323 BCE) – known in the West as 'The Great,' but in Iran as 'The Macedonian' – were assimilated into Persian culture as were the Arab armies who brought Islam with them in the seventh century CE, and the Mongols who attacked in the thirteenth century CE. Each of these groups of raiders initially created their own version of chaos to varying degrees and almost destroyed the country, but the people reclaimed the motherland in due course.

This was made possible first because of the sheer deep rootedness of the culture and secondly because the Iranian form of rule established by Cyrus the Great (590 – 529 BCE) was one based on a mutual set of obligations between the people and their rulers. Iranian people have always understood that if a king is not just and does not work in the interest of all, he must be deposed.

This spirit of rebellion against tyranny is also evident in Persian literature. As long as one thousand years ago, the poet who wrote the verses above, told the story of a mythical revolution against an evil king. The people protesting in Iran now, are taking much of their inspiration from Ferdowsi's poetry.

In other words, what has kept this heartland of the ancient Persian empire in once piece, has been the love and loyalty of its people for the motherland rather than submission to kings.

Thus, even from a young age, like other Iranians, I was raised with an affection for the land, the people, the culture, and the literature of Iran. This affection has never left me. It is a thing hard to describe but just the name of the country evokes feelings of deep pride and affinity in the heart. I still get the shudders when I think of the wild beasts of the Islamic Republic running loose in the streets of my homeland, laying ruin to society, and destroying lives.

The Islamic Republic has done its best to destroy the love of Iranians for their motherland and for all that is Persian, but they have been defeated time and time again. In the early years of the 1979 revolution, the Mullas in charge talked of Arabic becoming the language of Iran, destroying Persepolis, and banning traditional Persian festivities such as the Persian New Year. They distorted the content of history books in schools to downplay the achievements of Persian culture and to falsely ascribe heroic acts to themselves and their forebearers. They replaced original names of historic monuments to Islamic ones, and the list goes on.

*****

My family did not have any sympathy with the Islamic Republic. Leading up to the 1979 revolution, I had been brought up with my parents' moral principles. I knew it was out of the question to have a boyfriend, but also knew that education was good, and women were free to wear what they wanted – within reason. I also knew that men and women were as capable as each other. The women in my family were never into makeup or wearing the latest brands but they wore fashionable clothes and worked hard. None of them wore the hijab except my grandmothers and one aunt. I was raised in a house where both parents worked, and my father was often away so I was an independent teenager. The revolution did not change any of these beliefs and traits in me.

Once the revolution happened, we constantly lived in fear – a fear which I remember well although I was only ten years old at the time. The clearest manifestation of this fear was a recurring nightmare I used to have even long after I moved to Britain. I used to dream that I was out in public with no hijab. The sheer panic always made my heart race, and I would wake up in a cold sweat.

But compulsory hijab was not the only problem. Gradually, we lost all basic freedoms with bans or restrictions on food, music, dancing, parties, all arts, clothing, certain sports for women, and certain jobs for women amongst other things, culminating in my parents both losing their jobs because of their political beliefs.

This situation affected my parents in a way that it caused a clash of their lifelong love for Iran with the realisation that in this absolute lack of personal freedom, they had to do their best so that their children have better lives. Their solution was to send us abroad to study. So, people started leaving Iran because life was made unbearable, even dangerous for them by the Islamic Republic.

At the same time, the same dishonest, brutal behaviour of the Islamic Republic also gave Iranians a negative image abroad so that when they did emigrate from Iran, they were neither welcome nor understood in their new country. Being told to leave Iran by my parents was the beginning of my struggles with the issue of belonging.

When I was told that I was being sent to Britain to go to university, my first reaction was to refuse, but my parents decided it was for the best. I had no desire to marry an Englishman either or to stay in Britain. All of that just happened as I rode the waves of life. I never thought while I was growing up in Iran that I would end up being an immigrant so far from my homeland and for such a long time.

Once I started life in Britain, there were so many new things to learn that quite honestly, for the first few years, I did not think much about where I belonged to. After I got married, my allegiance was with my young family. I was close to the in-laws and saw my own parents once every few years including very few trips to Iran. But then there was the divorce, it shattered my attachment to the English family that I had known well for twenty years. It was then that I discovered what was meant by the English saying, 'Blood is thicker than water.'

It was as if I had been living a life pretending to myself that I belonged to the family unit that I had helped to create, but the feeling had clearly not been mutual. I tried to go back to my Iranian identity, but Iran was out of reach. The life I had built in Britain, my children and my job were firmly British. I decided that I was more British now than Iranian. Afterall, I had already spent most of my life in the UK. My naturalisation as a British citizen and my job as a civil servant gave me confidence that I had been accepted by Britain as one of its own. But again, this affiliation shattered years later through an incident at work when I realised that because of my Iranian origin, I was officially perceived as a liability by my employers. This second blow caused a crisis of identity within me that I am now trying to resolve by writing everything down.

*****

Looking back, as a child and later a teenager, I never questioned where my loyalties lay or which country I belonged to. But at the same time, after the 1979 revolution, knowing that the government did not represent the people of Iran, I hated the regime because its existence was creating a barrier between me and my Persian identity. By degrading Persian values and culture, the Islamic Republic was not allowing me to belong to Iran, and by creating a life of oppression, it forced me out of my homeland where I had always belonged. I now find myself in Britain struggling to define my own identity in order to satisfy that very human urge to belong to a place or a people.

The Islamic Republic took Iran away from its people. It took on our name and represented us in the guise of a legitimate government for 44 years. This is why one of the first slogans that people shouted in the streets of Iran in 2022 was 'We will fight! We will die! We will take back Iran!' They were asking for their homeland and their Persian identity to be restored to them.

I understand a friend to be someone who holds your hand,
In times of distress and desperation
Sa'di of Shiraz (1210 – 1292 CE)

دوست آن دانم که گیرد دست دوست
در پریشان حالی و درماندگی

The Kindness of Strangers

Living in this very different place has had its challenges but overall and with the benefit of hindsight, I am grateful to have been exposed to British culture because there is so much that is good and welcoming in this country.

There is a tradition of understated kindness to strangers in Britain which is genuine and deep rooted even if not practiced by all. The thoroughly English woman who sometimes took me in during university holidays on the recommendation of a friend, was one such example. Grace never charged me a penny for staying with her. She was like this with many people. Her house was open to all. Even when she was diagnosed with Alzheimer's disease and lived in a home for the elderly, she used to think that the other residents and the carers and nurses were her guests. She was the embodiment of her name.

When my son died at the age of one year and twenty days, following an accident at home, over five hundred people came to the funeral. I had asked anyone who wanted to help to just turn up to the funeral and they did. There were so many children from the primary school my other two children attended, that their red uniforms have been imprinted on my memory of that day. Families from the school also catered for the reception afterwards – again at no cost. My uncle who had come from Iran, remarked on how the Islamic Republic propaganda always says there is no solidarity in the West. One mum from the school whom I did not know well, embroidered a beautiful picture of Jesus holding an infant amongst clouds with the background of a white dove. This is 'love of thy neighbour' in its truest form.

When I was going through divorce, I used to take the children to church on Sundays on my own every other week. One time, when we were there, the children's father arrived with his new partner and his parents. They all sat together on the other side of the church. One of the mums from school came and sat next to me when she saw this. She said, 'I just want to sit with you. You can pretend to talk to me if you like, but I will understand if you don't want to do that.' Then she held my hand. I shall never forget that kindness.

I do have a British identity as well as an Iranian one. I will always queue in an orderly fashion. I have had to learn to reign in my frustration when I go to countries where people don't respect queues. Giving to charity has become second nature to me, another sound British habit. The British love of their pets is also moving. The unconditional love they have for animals, helps to ground them and is heart-warming to behold. A German vet I knew once told me that business is better in the UK than in Germany because people will bring their pet in and say, 'Please, keep him alive at any cost.'

Despite all that is said about British food, I do love roasts, pies, and fish and chips. It is a real skill to cook British food well. For one thing, I have never been able to master pastry making. When I go abroad, I miss British food and I miss Marmite.

I also love the various forms of British humour in all its sarcastic, dry, self-deprecating glory.

British and Irish ballads, create deep emotions in me. I know most nursery rhymes by heart and love the British pop music of the 1960s and the 1970s.

*****

So, yes, I have found some good friends and I have assimilated, but it has not been an easy ride. There have been those who do not care to learn about who I am or what my story is. I have either decided to educate such people or have given up on them with a residue of rejection in my heart. By far the most challenging aspect of trying to belong however, has been sifting through the good and the not-so-good people I have come across, and trying not to tar everyone with the same brush.

A strange land is not a place where people do not know you.
It is a state whereby loved ones choose to forget about you.

Fazel Nazari (1979 -)

اینکه مردم نشناسند تو را غربت نیست،
غربت آن است که یاران ببرند از یادت

The Misunderstood Altruist

One way in which immigrants can be classified is by dividing them into two types. The first type is those who move to another country for personal reasons and are able to go back and forth to their homeland whenever they wish; say for the summer holidays or to see relatives. The second type are exiled immigrants; refugees or people who either can't go back or only go back if they must; say for the death of a relative or the marriage of another. Many Iranians in the diaspora, including me, fall into the second category.

Of all the issues that I have had to come to terms with as an immigrant, that of 'belonging' is most problematic. When you come from a culture with such strong affinity with the homeland, it is hard to simply transfer that love to another place. Yet, since I arrived here, I knew that I could not live in Britain in a state of 'unbelonging' either. Especially when I finally realised there was no prospect of me going back to live in Iran.

If we accept that love is what binds people together, the emotional plight of the exiled immigrant becomes more apparent to us. Once a person is torn from their roots and loved ones, many emotional bonds are severed or at best damaged. New connections must be formed in the new country. But it can be difficult to create the same binding feelings with people of a different culture especially when exiled immigrants generally come from countries that are culturally dissimilar.

*****

When I arrived in the Britain of the mid-1980s on my own – still a teenager, I was determined to assimilate. Within a few years, I could fit in and out of my two cultures seamlessly and I was proud of that.

But in my heart, I did not understand this new way of life. Subconsciously, in the absence of the people who had loved me unconditionally, in an effort to belong, I transferred a selfless love to strangers. So, with the passing of years, I lost the sense of what it was to be myself and lived to please others. It took a long while for me to link this behaviour with the course that my life had taken.

I once read somewhere that people who give others lavish gifts, are saying, 'This is how much you should love me.' I did not have much money, but I used to make beautiful things for people. I used to spend hours embroidering or painting or looking for exactly the right gift for someone, most of those people have gone on living their separate lives. It is wrong to give gifts with the hope of a return of favours, but I was subconsciously doing that. That is something I don't do anymore. I have learnt to recognise real affection and to give gifts to those who truly care about me without expecting anything in return.

Where romantic love was concerned, years went by before I realised that it was dangerous to have roots in a culture where you were taught to stay in a relationship forever, while living in a place where you had no roots. You were basically left vulnerable when faced with people who were seeking someone amenable to control.

Matters were further complicated for me because my own family was not good at emotional support. Communication was so scarce that at times it felt like they had forgotten about me.

My family were also anglophiles. They had a subconscious belief that English people were superior to Iranians. Although Iran has never been a colony, the British were highly involved in the oil industry in the part of Iran where my parents lived. My parents had grown up seeing entitled colonial officials and oil workers around them and were impressed by the British. They happily approved of my marriage to a British man and were so proud of their son-in-law that

I was left feeling isolated and unable to tell them of the unhappiness in my marriage.

Difficulties with long-distance communication in those days did not help. In our world today, the freedom to call people across the world for free has linked many immigrants with their original families. I fully appreciate the people who designed this technology. They have provided a service to humankind.

Despite such advances in communication, for exiled immigrants who generally travel across continents and live in countries with significantly different cultures, it is still harder to have that feeling of affinity with their new country. It is easier for a German or Spanish person to fit into British culture because they have the same religion, similar culture, and live in equally free states. Their alphabets are the same and their languages are closely linked. Europeans living in Britain are also generally there by choice. They are not exiles.

Another issue with Iran is that the Islamic Republic heavily censors all art, music, movies, literature, and news. The content of most programmes from Iran is so twisted to fit the 'ideal' of the government, that it does not represent the true face of Persian culture or the real Iranian way of life. I have mostly avoided all such contact with Iran since I arrived in Britain. At first, I could not access any media in Iran anyway, but when satellite and internet links were established, I quickly found out that I had nothing in common with this 'official' image of Iran.

So, understanding and fitting into the British way of life was one challenge but another was accepting that I was often the only representation of true Iran that I could offer my British friends. Every now and then people would tell me about some Iranian film they had seen and ask questions like 'Do women wear hijab even in bed?' or 'Why don't you wear the hijab?' I then had to go into my full explanation of how hijab was enforced on women in Iran and how the films do not represent Iran. It was exhausting at times to hear yourself repeat the same defensive arguments. So, I generally stopped talking to some British acquaintances about Iran or my life before arriving in the UK because it was easier that way.

*****

As an immigrant, to have that sense of belonging, you do need friends in the new country. In order not to feel like an outcast, you need loved ones around you in your new home. But finding friends who understand all aspects of your character, especially when you are isolated and existing representations of your culture are negative, is not easily achieved.

The only people who fully understand you are those who have the same life experiences or people who take the time to learn about your homeland. As I have said, I have been blessed with many such friends although it has taken me a long time to find them. With these good friends who remember me and look out for me and after close to forty years of living in the UK, I should feel like I belong in Britain, but I don't. This feeling bothers me. That is why I decided to write this essay.

I am a ruin inside, but I appear to prosper.
My heart is a city of silent people, while my eyes scream.

Lyrics from Yusuf-e Gomgashteh; Sung by Sattar

از درون همه ویرانم، اما ظاهرم آباد
شهر خاموشان است قلبم، تو چشمهام پُر فریاد

The Pitfalls of Assimilation

As with everyone else, the dynamics of my parents' relationship with each other and with the opposite sex also affected my relationships with men. Once I left home, although I was alone, I did not look to men for emotional support or love. That was not how my mother was with my father. On the other hand, my mother had good male friends, so I looked to men for friendship and fun and interestingly also looked at them as equals. This meant that I generally got on well with men but did not have many romantic partners.

Since my mid-teens, I had an idea that the partner I was looking for had to be different to my father, not the aggressive type anyway. He would have to be a man who would help around the house and would treat my children well – although I had not quite worked out the details of this latter condition. The subtleties of choosing a man who would be kind and empathise also eluded me. I did not know that being mutually kind and understanding is fundamental to the survival of any relationship.

Another misconception I had was that I thought all English people had grown up with universally accepted feminist values. I did not realise that in fact my mother, who had a career as a high school teacher amongst other things, was a far more liberated woman than many women of her generation in Britain. In the Britain of the 1980s, although Margaret Thatcher was Prime Minister, it was quite common for people of my age to have mothers who were housewives. The mothers of my friends at university generally did not work. Englishmen too were by extension not necessarily feminist. You cannot generalise fully about any society.

Just as there are close-minded people in Iran, so they also exist everywhere else. Anyone can use cultural or religious reasons to dominate others if they are that way inclined. Meanwhile, I had come out of Iran thinking that all the prejudice I had suffered was because of the religion and the regime restrictions peculiar to Iran. This idea made me feel dangerously safe in Britain. It made me trust too much.

Furthermore, the inexperience of my youth made me judge people according to how outwardly aggressive they were. So, my world was divided into the nice people who did not shout or act out violently and the bad people who did. My childhood heavily supported this bipolar division. I had grown up in a house with a volatile father and a long-suffering mother.

I did not know that my real challenge was to find people who do not seek to control or manipulate but rather are kind and respect one's choices in life. Such people can be calm and quiet or not.

Herein lies one of the subtleties of being displaced. Control manifests itself differently in different cultures. My experience has been that generally, Iranians are more obvious when trying to exert their dominance. By contrast, the English are more subtle and polite about convincing you that they are right. Not being able to spot subtle control can drag one into unloving relationships as you confuse this control with love and protection. Cultural awareness is partly about being aware of the different modes of expression in different cultures.

*****

So, this is how it happened that when I arrived in Britain, operating on an original default setting, I carried on being wary of outwardly aggressive people and gravitated towards people who appeared even tempered. I was not even aware of passive aggression as a concept back then.

This was how I came to have some very good, gentle friends but it was also how in my closest relationships, I trusted people who did not have my best interests at heart. After much soul searching, I see that because I was torn from my original home, I was afraid of being abandoned. This made me too compliant when in close relationships. Add to that the concept of not being able to interpret emotions in different cultures and you get the dangerous cocktail that I was subconsciously imbibing.

In my quest for love and belonging, being displaced had placed other challenges in my path as well as the ones I had grown up with.

*****

My young age was clearly a disadvantage. Furthermore, aside from the different cultural setting that I have touched upon, I did not appreciate my own unhappiness because although as a child I knew that there were loving family members around me, I had felt uncomfortable and unhappy through living in an unhappy home. This uneasy feeling was the norm to me. I did not question it. You may think it a simple case of a lack of self-esteem, but it is more than that. When a child learns to tiptoe around angry adults, she is not aware of what it means to be accepted, loved, and respected for who she is by the people closest to her.

Between the aggressive and non-aggressive modes of control described earlier, the common denominator was that uneasy feeling inside that I had always co-existed with. I had no understanding that to be truly happy, I had to strive to be with people who eliminated that feeling in me.

By gravitating towards that familiar but unhealthy feeling, where intimacy was concerned, I fell into a pattern of forming bad relationships. When I step back to look at my past, I wonder how many times I fell in with people who perpetuated my feeling of not being good enough.

Based on my own experience, I believe that sometimes it is through subconsciously seeking the wrong company in their desperation to belong, that some immigrants may perpetuate their existing feelings of inadequacy.

Whether immigrant or not, if you come from a disturbed, compromised background, you may end up seeking 'the familiar' thus repeating the vicious cycle of feeling unwanted. At the same time, your most ardent wish is to belong. In your determination to achieve this belonging, you make further compromises when it comes to being yourself. In this respect the experience of those who immigrate as a family and most importantly a loving family, is very different to mine.

So it was that even though this made me unhappy, I adapted my behaviour to fit in with my environment. I often excused bad behaviour by telling myself this was a 'cultural difference.' The other party was particularly successful in fooling me if they explained their behaviour in a very calm, civilised way. One instance of this was when a partner spent an inordinate time with his ex-girlfriend in my company while ignoring me.

When I mentioned this, he explained this away as 'no big deal.' He had been friends with her for nearly two years after all, which was a much longer time than he had known me. Friends needed to catch up with each other from time to time... I assumed that was the British way of doing things.

Had he shouted and called me names, perhaps I would have seen matters differently.

You may say people like this exist in any culture. Any narcissist can gaslight their co-dependent partner. My quarrel with one aspect of English culture is that in my experience it abhors expressions of anger and emotional outbursts and so can normalise this kind of 'rational justification' as an acceptable mode of operation.

One result of all this was that in time, as I assimilated into English culture, my Iranian identity faded into the shadows. I continuously adjusted my behaviour to appear unperturbed while I was screaming inside. I began to feel like a ruin inside while on the outside, I seemed content. Within my closest relationships, only occasionally, the expressive Iranian girl would burst out when life became too difficult. I was then made to feel bad for shouting or swearing or being overly emotional.

If this is what the famous English reserve does for people, it can't be a good thing.

This switching of roles happens to an extent to all displaced people. Even people who have not moved into a different culture can behave differently depending on the person they are addressing.

*****

I have always been aware that even my best English friends don't fully know my Iranian side. I feel equally different to Iranians who have not lived in Britain. Despite this, I have formed genuine, loving relationships with people in both these groups. It is with my British Iranian friends however, that I feel most myself. It's a matter of shared experiences.

Many of these experiences are amusing and concern the contrasting practices in both cultures. I remember chatting with a British-Iranian friend whose husband is German. She was talking about visiting her in-laws in Germany. Now, Iranians generally have their main meal at lunchtime and have a siesta afterwards if they can. My friend and I were laughing about the German – and British – tendency to go 'for a walk' after a meal. She was saying, 'Why would you want to do that? And what is worse, they are not going to any place in particular. They are just walking for the sake of it!' Whereas this is a healthy habit, the idea of it still makes me laugh. It is so much the opposite to the Iranian way of life.

British Iranians also always wonder out loud about the 'bizarre' British practice of having separate cold and hot taps. 'How are you supposed to get the correct temperature? Just cup your hands under each tap and go to-and-fro between them until you get it right? What a waste of time and energy!'

Then it is the 'bubbles on dishes that don't get washed up!' Iranians are obsessive about rinsing washed, soapy dishes but not so the British.

By way of contrast, a dual national friend once told me that as soon as he got in a taxi in Iran, the driver said, 'So, you live abroad?' When my friend asked how he knew this, the guy said, 'Because you fastened your seatbelt.'

Years ago, we had a British visitor in Iran. She spent a lot of time taking photographs of the backsides of Iranian sheep because they are of the fat-tailed variety. We found this amusing. As amusing as her efforts to try and sit on the floor while she ate. Once she even ended up lying on her side.

The weather is a whole topic on its own. My Iranian side loves rain as a giver of life. The British woman in me, hates it when it rains. I remember speaking with my mother on the phone. I said, 'How's the weather in Tehran?' She said, 'Fantastic! It's been raining for a week.' I had to do a double take and stare at the receiver in my hand before I twigged and changed cultures in my head.

He said: Thou who appear vexed, where art thou from?
I said: I am a stranger from the city of acquaintances.

Ghazal extract of Khwaju-ye Kermani (1280-1352 BCE)

گفتا تو از کجایی کآشفته می نمایی؟
گفتم منم غریبی از شهر آشنایی

Identity

There is an Iranian play which dates to 1966. It is called Shahr-e Ghesseh or 'The City of Stories.' The play is a satire based on the Tehran of the 1960s. All the characters in the play are animals. They have jobs that suit their stereotypes in Persian folklore. Interestingly, the fox is a Mulla.

A stranger arrives in the city. He is an elephant with a long trunk and two large tusks. He is essentially the embodiment of one of the many thousands of country folk who were coming to the big city looking for work. The inhabitants of the city do not like his name which is Fil – elephant in Persian. They do not like his looks either. In order to fit in, it is suggested to him that he should cut his trunk into many chunks and give the bits away to the people watching. His tusks are then also removed and put on his head. His name is then also changed to Manuchehr – meaning 'a face like paradise'. Only then is he deemed acceptable.

I have identified with this elephant at times. That is usually when I look at myself from the outside and wonder if an Iranian saw me interacting with English people, how unfamiliar I would be to them. How when I am with Iranians who live in Iran, I feel like an imposter. I try to be like them, but they know, and I know that I am different. 'Changing my face' doesn't quite work in either culture.

There is a difference however, I do feel more understood by Iranians – even those living in Iran - than the British – except for my closest family and friends of course.

Given the pervasive influence of British culture in global media and literature, Iranians are far more familiar with everything British whereas British people generally know little about Iran. I know this from the number of times I have had to explain myself and Iran to the British. The most worrying aspect of this is when people have a fear of you as an Iranian which you must work to dispel. I remember British friends who when they first found out I was from Iran, looked visibly shocked.

So, Britain is that 'city of acquaintances' for me. I don't appear quite 'native' to Iranians, but they are familiar with the place I have lived in as an adult. I am a stranger to them, but they have a better feel for who I am. I, on the other hand, have been both an observer and an actor in both cultures. In that sense, I am not as obvious a misfit as the elephant in Shahr-e Qesseh. I still look Iranian, and I have a Persian name.

There is a city beyond the seas,
In which all windows open to Realisation

Sohrab Sepehri (1928 – 1980)

پشت دریاها شهری است
که در آن پنجره ها رو به تجلی بازست

A Hierarchy of Needs

Wherever a person lives, they need to feel that they belong to a wider group. Humans are social animals. Feeling alienated makes us suffer mentally and physically. That suffering will hinder us from achieving our full potential and giving our most to the society in which we live. A society which is hostile to its own people, is doing itself a disservice and is ultimately doomed.

Abraham Maslow of course describes the importance of 'love and belonging' in his 'Theory of Human Motivation.'

According to Maslow's Hierarchy of Needs, to achieve their full potential, a person must have the following needs met, starting with the most basic: Physiological, safety, love and belonging, and esteem.

The 'love and belonging' tier contains friendship, intimacy, family, and a sense of connection. In my case, as I strive towards realising my full potential, which is just visible through the windows in that city beyond the seas, I am increasingly aware that I am stuck, even immobilised on this tier. Without love and belonging, true self-esteem, respect for oneself, a sense of freedom, and ultimately fulfilment, will elude us. A displaced person, whether an isolated, exiled immigrant or someone with damaged family ties – more than others, needs this sense of belonging to truly thrive.

I know that friendship, intimacy, family, and sense of connection have been compromised in my life because of my status as an exiled immigrant and my family background. Since I became aware of this, I have been able to analyse the past and try to amend the future.

*****

Unachievable Expectations

A sense of being loved goes hand in hand with the feeling of belonging. If people say they love you but, in their actions, they don't make you feel like you belong to their family or their friendship group, then they are being dishonest either just with you or with themselves as well. On the other hand, if you are truly treated as part of a group, then you feel accepted and 'loved' or 'cared for' by them.

This reciprocal relationship between love and belonging has been a key discovery for me. I have been in many one-way relationships when an imaginary 'love' or 'belonging' has been present. These have ended in disappointment at best, and heartbreak at worst.

As a ten-year-old, back in Iran, I used to wonder about what 'love' was. I used to think, 'How do people know that they love each other?' Now that I have had time to look back, I know that those feelings came from a sense of 'not belonging.' My parents, although they were both educated, secular and outwardly westernised, longed for a male child as is the custom in many Muslim societies. We were three sisters. To make matters worse, their firstborn had been a boy but was stillborn. Both parents often voiced their disappointment at not having a son. All three of us knew that we were not welcomed into this world with open arms.

So, there was love in my family but there was not enough of it, and it was often conditional. All three of us had to prove that although we were not male, we could achieve more than any son our parents would have had. My older sister was under most pressure, but we all felt this expectation to succeed. We knew that if we didn't hit the targets set for us, we would be seriously admonished. In happy families, children just feel loved no matter what they do. Not having that, made me just operate on a 'work to succeed' basis. This upbringing also meant that I grew up to be a people pleaser. It was this character trait that I later transferred to strangers that I met in Britain. Although I do remember instances of unconditional love as a child because I had mostly experienced conditional love, being displaced exacerbated that trait in me.

So, I set about being polite and respectful in all circumstances. My mantra was 'respond not react.' I decided to educate people rather than get angry. I let a lot of offhand comments pass me by and smiled at people who asked me if we had clouds in Iran or if our houses were made of mud.

There were exceptions when I couldn't keep quiet. One of my worst arguments with an English partner was that he wouldn't accept that the American pronunciation of 'Iran' was wrong. It got to me that I couldn't even have an opinion about how the name of my own homeland should be pronounced. Another time, when my boss told me he was surprised at how good my English was when I had written a letter of commendation for an employee, I found myself telling him that I was a British citizen and had lived in Britain for all my adult life and that I was not a 'crazy flag burner.'

But ultimately, just as I could never become a boy to have the full approval of my parents, I could not become a native British person and feel accepted in Britain. The most innocent reminder of this is every time I am asked where I am from, and I give my usual sentence: 'I'm originally from Iran but I have lived here since I was seventeen.' An extreme example was when I had worked as a civil servant for 20 years but my relationship with a colleague was undermined by our employer because of my 'nationality status.' I fought for five years to clear my name on that occasion but to no avail. I was still considered a liability by my employer because the regime I took refuge from is evil; this being the reason I left Iran in the first place.

I have spent much of my time in Britain defending my heritage. The dehumanisation of Iranians by Western media has not helped. Repeated uprisings by Iranian people in opposition to the Islamic Republic went ignored until the people of Iran did not give the West a chance to ignore them. For me personally, the uprising that started in September 2022 is a ray of hope that I can one day return to Iran and help to rebuild the country. Then maybe, just maybe, I will get back a more complete sense of belonging to one place rather than half belonging to two places.

*****

As life stories of exiled immigrants go, mine is a stable, even privileged one. All humans have their emotional baggage from childhood. The issue with exiled immigrants is that once they are displaced, other hardships are added to their original load. It is in the interest of their new country to help alleviate the extra emotional burdens of being displaced. Afterall, if they are not fully accepted in the new country, their mental and hence physical health will suffer – a situation that can only be to the disadvantage of their country of residence. A healthy society should strive to help all its citizens achieve self-actualisation.

The best way to ensure that this happens however is through good governance including correct education. I strongly believe that if a government does not put policies in place to educate its native population and to protect the rights of immigrants, it is the state apparatus that carries the main responsibility for disharmony and suffering in society and not the people.

Sustenance arrives from God's table with every guest. Whoever becomes our guest, is also our host.

Sa'eb Tabrizi (1592 – 1676 CE)

رزق می آید به پای مهمان، از خوان غیب
میزبان ماست، هرکس می شود مهمان ما

Philoxenia

We would all love to live in a utopia where all windows open to fulfilment. Immigrants, more than the native population of a place, have a need to feel like they belong there to fulfil their potential and be of value to the host country. So, you would think by now, as a species, we would have figured this out and would have developed a culture which is welcoming to displaced newcomers.

Philoxenia is a Greek word which has been translated as 'hospitality' in the New Testament. It in fact means 'loving strangers.' Most religions encourage their followers to be hospitable and yet, in the English language at least, we are more familiar with the word 'Xenophobia', the fear of strangers.

How has it happened that Xenophobia has gained in strength and far from 'loving strangers' many Western governments brood over the threats and risks of immigration?

I have a specific experience as an Iranian immigrant in Britain. This experience has made me come to certain conclusions about how British society could prosper and how past mistakes can be rectified to manifest this prosperity.

As I see it, cultural assimilation is good, but it works at its best with humility from all involved. It should be a matter of picking up what is best from each other's cultures rather than making everyone comply with the culture of the host country. The attitude that dictates all immigrants should copy all aspects of British culture, assumes a superiority of all British values irrespective of their actual merit. I would like to suggest that in the matter of emotional expression for one thing, English culture can benefit from expanding its horizons.

The class system in Britain is also something that immigrant communities and the great majority of non-immigrants are better off without. This is especially because I see the class system as closely connected with slavery and colonialism. As I understand it, before the age of European empires, slavery was practised but without singling out a particular race. Certain tribes, kingdoms, or empires used to take anyone captive during various wars and the captives would be sometimes sold as slaves, or pirates or other bandits would kidnap anyone at hand and sell them as slaves.

This was the norm until European empires started a dangerous ideology which justified slavery or the abuse of other 'races' by explicitly or implicitly declaring their inferiority to the 'white' race. This was philoxenia being replaced by xenophobia.

The class system in Britain has exacerbated this situation further by implying that a certain section of the 'white' population is superior to the rest as well - another layer of separation. What is more, over the years, the flames of racism have been fanned by those in the upper classes who saw it in their interest to keep both working-class British people and colonial British subjects, poor to maintain their position in society and their wealth.

In the years following WWII, once the colonies were disbanded and children of colonised people arrived in Britain to help rebuild the country, the upper classes presided over conflict between the new arrivals and their native British subjects. While frustrated with their own disadvantages, British middle- and working-class people found it difficult to direct their anger at those in charge and instead, racism took hold as a way of venting frustration.

We have come a long way from those days, but it often appears that the class system is still ruling supreme and that is disturbing. In Britain at least, I feel that this system encourages Xenophobia by its implied suggestion that, to quote George Orwell in Animal Farm, 'All animals are equal, but some are more equal than others.'

People who are unfulfilled will seek ways to belong to something else once the place they or their parents took refuge in, rejects them. This is where education has the potential to save the day.

Oh! Holy man, for how long thou will continue deceiving people as if they were children,
With promises of apple orchards, honey, and milk?

Hafez of Shiraz (1325 – 1390 CE)

چو طفلان تا کی ای زاهد فریبی
به سیب بوستان و شهد و شیرم

The Extreme Consequence of Unbelonging

The poem above refers to the belief that rivers of honey and milk run in paradise. Hafez was a poet who challenged religious institutions but praised spirituality. It is interesting that now, over six centuries since these words were written, Islamist organisations use these same promises – not to mention the seventy-two virgins awaiting every man in paradise - to recruit young people all over the world.

These extreme religious groups often target children of immigrants and offer them a link to their identity, to the colour of their skin, and to the different religious customs they have been raised with. In the absence of strong links with their heritage, these children hang on to religion in order to belong and be accepted by 'a group.' Some may have also experienced racism and bullying at school. My own thoughts about radicalisation first took shape when my half-English son was asked by another pupil at his school whether he was related to Bin Laden. My son took this in his stride because although he doesn't speak Persian, he knows a lot about Iran and Persian history and culture. This incident made me angry of course but it also made me think that other children needed this armour.

Speaking for myself, I clearly remember being ten years old and having a good think about what kind of person I wanted to be when I grew up. My conclusion was that I had to watch my friends and their parents in my search for role models. I decided I couldn't just emulate my parents because they didn't always treat me well. This is a human reaction. If you are living in a hostile place, you know you can't find kindred spirits among your immediate peers, then you go searching for another peer group. You don't always find the right set of people either. Sometimes, as long as the new guys treat you better, you feel wanted and decide to stay.

In Britain, education in schools generally follows the same pattern of teaching every child almost exclusively a carefully selected history and literature of the British Isles. I believe that such educational policies have inadvertently led to the radicalisation of young people among immigrant communities – as well as implying the superiority of all things British.

Children of immigrants who do not learn to read the language of their parents or sometimes don't speak that language either, feel alienated at school because they cannot identify with the historical figures or the literature that they are reading about. Furthermore, their native British classmates often have little knowledge of other cultures and so can assume their own as being most important or 'better.'

If the model of assimilation based on highlighting the positive aspects of every culture were to be followed, every child would have a source of pride at school that others would also learn to respect.

Immigrant families who encourage their children to conform in the new country and aspire to become 'just like' or 'even better' than the host, put their children under unrealistic pressure. Trying to become something you are not can cause an identity crisis much like the elephant of Shahr-e Qesseh, you end up not knowing your own name and you cannot recognise yourself in the mirror.

If British schools taught the history of the Mughal Empire or African kingdoms and threw in the myths and legends of ancient Persia or China in literature lessons, all children would be educated about world cultures. Immigrant children would have a source of pride and belonging, and non-immigrants would understand better that no culture is superior to others or more worthy to be studied. The study of a realistic history of the British Empire is also much needed.

Some have seen the creation of 'faith schools' as a way to meet the cultural needs of immigrant populations and religious minorities. As someone whose own children went to a Catholic school but has now grown to realise that religion is a strictly personal matter, I don't believe that these schools are necessary or helpful. To my mind, any institution that segregates populations is divisive. By focusing on our differences rather than our common humanity, we stop cultural assimilation in its best form.

These are all personal opinions. As a teacher of language and culture, I have seen these principles work at first hand. Although the great majority of my students are non-immigrants, I have seen the windows of Realisation open wide for them as they have learnt about Iran. With this education, their pre-conceived ideas about Iran have also changed and their respect for the people, culture and history of Iran has increased.

Hey! You people, who are sat on the beach, joyful and laughing!
Someone is drowning in the water.
Someone is desperately flailing their limbs.

Nima Youshij (1895 – 1960)

آی آدمها که بر ساحل نشسته شاد و خندانید!
یک نفر در آب دارد می سپارد جان
یک نفر دارد که دست و پای دائم می زند

Separating 'The Politics' from 'The People'

My experience has been that since I arrived in Britain, I perceived myself as equal to the people I met, but in time I realised that there were some who considered themselves better than me because of their family background. This is while these particular people did not know anything about my family background, because they had never been to Iran or seen my parents or talked with me about my life in Iran.

In time I realised that there was such a thing as the entitled social classes in Britain. When I arrived in Cambridge to go to university, I knew I was going to a good university but knew nothing whatsoever that the place had a reputation for attracting children of the rich and famous. What is interesting is that although I heard that certain people were related to certain personalities or aristocratic families, I never sought their friendship. They were just not my type. I do think that this sentiment worked both ways. They were also not interested in people who didn't frequent certain social circles.

The friends I did find were all interesting and fun and the best ones were kind too. They were generally of middle-class families like my own in Iran. A few had achieved amazing feats by being the first person in their family to make it to university.

So, to go back to my original reason for writing this piece, I now see that the root of the 'unbelonging' that I feel in Britain is 'The Politics' and not 'The People.' Whoever we are, we can always choose our friends, there will always be rich people and not-so rich people. There will always be people we get on with and those we don't. For immigrants however, navigating the choppy waters of a host nation ensconced in only a limited version of its own history and culture, is an alienating experience.

As a mother, and because I have always loved history, I took great interest in my children's history lessons. My knowledge of history before I had children was mainly Middle Eastern with a bias towards Iran. I knew of key points in British history but was really looking forward to learning more through the children. The experience was a disappointment as year after year, they only seemed to learn about the wives of Henry VIII or the two World Wars of the modern era.

None of this is new. It has been recognised that the teaching of culture in schools is of high importance in our globalised world. But the British government has been slow in catching up. As a result, not only the children are missing out, but their parents who could be exposed to a sound cultural content through the children, are being deprived of this learning.

A part of me also thinks that it has been in the interest of the British upper classes for this cultural limitation to continue, or rather, they may not seek to pursue it as the lives of the lower strata in society including refugees and immigrants do not really affect them. As politics in Britain is still very much an upper-class domain, perhaps it is not surprising that a move towards further equalising social classes does not seem to have gone ahead with any real purpose.

*****

Meanwhile in Iran, people have taken to the streets to overthrow an evil government and make it known that they don't stand for the values of the Islamic Republic. A large part of this latest revolution for 'Woman – Life – Freedom' is attending to the needs of women, immigrants, particularly Afghan immigrants, native ethnic groups, the poor, children, and LGBTQ groups. The people are dragging their country into the 21st century with all their might.

They are also asking for a secular, democratic government as a replacement for the Islamic Republic.

They do not want any particular section of society to have a monopoly over politics in Iran ever again.

Not before long, Britain may be looking at Iran for inspiration so that merit and not the accident of birth will be the measure of a person's capability as a politician. Or perhaps, once Iran is free, British tourists will visit the country and educate themselves about Iranians. Either way, those of us who live here – if indeed we decide to remain after the fall of the Islamic Republic – may finally feel better understood.

Other books by this author and available on Amazon:

Transcultural (paperback and ebook)

Aberu (ebook)

Maman (ebook)

Affinity (ebook)

Printed by Amazon Italia Logistica S.r.l.
Torrazza Piemonte (TO), Italy